IDAHO

The Gem State

BY
JOHN HAMILTON

Abdo & Daughters

An imprint of Abdo Publishing | abdopublishing.com

abdopublishing.com

Published by ABDO Publishing, a division of ABDO, PO Box 398166, Minneapolis, Minnesota 55439. Copyright © 2017 by Abdo Consulting Group, Inc. International copyrights reserved in all countries. No part of this book may be reproduced in any form without written permission from the publisher. ABDO & Daughters™ is a trademark and logo of ABDO Publishing.

Printed in the United States of America, North Mankato, Minnesota.
012016
092016

THIS BOOK CONTAINS
RECYCLED MATERIALS

Editor: Sue Hamilton   **Contributing Editor:** Bridget O'Brien
Graphic Design: Sue Hamilton
Cover Art Direction: Candice Keimig   **Cover Photo Selection:** Neil Klinepier
Cover Photo: iStock
Interior Images: Alamy, AP, Boise Hawks, Corbis, Dreamstime, Estate of Edgar Rice Burroughs, Getty, Glow Images, Granger, History in Full Color-Restoration/Colorization, Idaho Falls Chukars, Idaho Museum of Natural History/Idaho State University, Idaho Potato Commission, Idaho Stampede, Idaho State Historical Society, Independence National Historical Park/C.W. Peale artist, Idaho Steelheads, iStock, Library of Congress, Minden Pictures, Mile High Maps, Mountain High Maps, National Park Service, North Wind Picture Archives, One Mile Up, Port of Lewiston, Science Source, Special Olympics, U.S. Army, Wikimedia.

Statistics: *State and City Populations*, U.S. Census Bureau, July 1, 2014 estimates; *Land and Water Area*, U.S. Census Bureau, 2010 Census, MAF/TIGER database; *State Temperature Extremes*, NOAA National Climatic Data Center; *Climatology and Average Annual Precipitation*, NOAA National Climatic Data Center, 1980-2015 statewide averages; *State Highest and Lowest Points*, NOAA National Geodetic Survey.

Websites: To learn more about the United States, visit booklinks.abdopublishing.com. These links are routinely monitored and updated to provide the most current information available.

Cataloging-in-Publication Data

Names: Hamilton, John, 1959- author.
Title: Idaho / by John Hamilton.
Description: Minneapolis, MN : Abdo Publishing, [2016] | The United States of America | Includes index.
Identifiers: LCCN 2015957540 | ISBN 9781680783148 (print) | ISBN 9781680774184 (ebook)
Subjects: LCSH: Idaho--Juvenile literature.
Classification: DDC 979.6--dc23
LC record available at http://lccn.loc.gov/2015957540

CONTENTS

THE GEM STATE

There's a lot more to Idaho than potatoes. The state is also famous for its wide-open spaces. It is a land filled with unspoiled wilderness. Rugged mountain ranges and forests teeming with wildlife sprawl over more than half the state.

The heart of Idaho is centered on small farming towns. Crops grow on about one-fifth of the state. Potatoes are a big cash crop, but so are wheat, sugar beets, and barley. Although small-town life is unhurried, there is plenty of urban excitement in Idaho's bustling cities such as Boise, or ski resort towns such as Sun Valley.

Nobody really knows how Idaho got its name. In years past, many thought it was a Shoshone Native American word that meant "gem of the mountains." That turned out to be untrue. But Idaho is a land filled with natural treasures, from emerald-colored forests to deep, sapphire-tinted mountain lakes. Idaho truly lives up to its nickname: The Gem State.

McGowan Peak rises 9,860 feet (3,005 m) above sea level in Idaho's Sawtooth Range.

QUICK FACTS

Name: Idaho was thought to be a Native American word that meant "gem of the mountains." It may also have been named after a steamship that regularly traveled up the Columbia River.

State Capital: Boise, population 216,282

Date of Statehood: July 3, 1890 (43rd state)

Population: 1,634,464 (39th-most populous state)

Area (Total Land and Water): 83,569 square miles (216,443 sq km), 14th-largest state

Largest City: Boise, population 216,282

Nickname: The Gem State

Motto: *Esto Perpetua* (Let it be forever)

State Bird: Mountain Bluebird

State Flower: Syringa

State Gemstone: Star Garnet

State Tree: Western White Pine

State Song: "Here We Have Idaho"

Highest Point: Borah Peak, 12,662 feet (3,859 m)

Lowest Point: 710 feet (216 m) on the Snake River

Average July High Temperature: 82°F (28°C)

Record High Temperature: 118°F (48°C), in Orofino on July 28, 1934

Average January Low Temperature: 16°F (-9°C)

Record Low Temperature: -60°F (-51°C), in Island Park on January 18, 1943

Average Annual Precipitation: 24 inches (61 cm)

Number of U.S. Senators: 2

Number of U.S. Representatives: 2

U.S. Postal Service Abbreviation: ID

QUICK FACTS

GEOGRAPHY

Some say Idaho is shaped like an old logger's boot. Its narrow panhandle juts up to the north. At its narrowest, it is only about 45 miles (72 km) across. The southern part of Idaho is much wider. It measures about 305 miles (491 km) from east to west. From north to south, the state is 479 miles (771 km) long.

Six states border Idaho. Washington and Oregon are to the west. To the east are Montana and Wyoming. Nevada and Utah are on Idaho's southern border. The Canadian province of British Columbia borders Idaho to the north.

Northern Idaho's panhandle is filled with beautiful mountains, forests, and lakes.

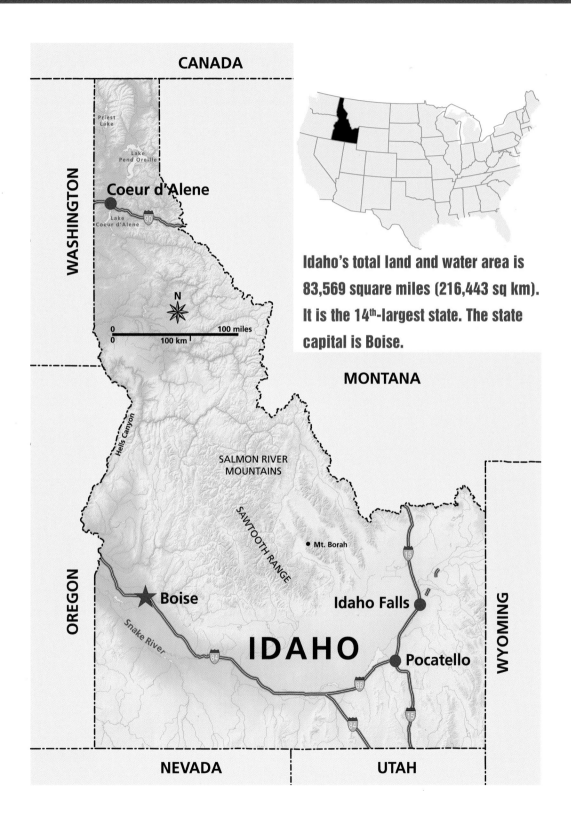

CANADA

Priest Lake

Lake Pend Oreille

WASHINGTON

Coeur d'Alene

Lake Coeur d'Alene

N

0   100 miles
0   100 km

Idaho's total land and water area is 83,569 square miles (216,443 sq km). It is the 14th-largest state. The state capital is Boise.

MONTANA

Hells Canyon

SALMON RIVER MOUNTAINS

SAWTOOTH RANGE

Mt. Borah

OREGON

Boise

Idaho Falls

IDAHO

Snake River

Pocatello

WYOMING

NEVADA   UTAH

The Snake River forms part of Idaho's western border between the states of Washington and Oregon.

Idaho contains about 4.8 million acres (1.9 million ha) of untouched wilderness lands. They include mountains, lakes, rivers, and gorges. Only Alaska and California have more wilderness.

The northern panhandle is filled with tree-lined mountains, green hillsides, and deep mountain lakes. Moving south into central Idaho, the land becomes even more mountainous. There are dozens of subranges of the Rocky Mountains. The most rugged include the Bitterroot, Sawtooth, Clearwater, and Salmon River Mountains. Borah Peak is in the Lost River Mountain Range. It is Idaho's highest point, soaring to 12,662 feet (3,859 m). Idaho's lowest point is on the Snake River, where it joins the Clearwater River along the border of Washington. That point is just 710 feet (216 m) above sea level.

In southern Idaho, the Snake River winds its way east to west across the state. The ground here is more level than in the mountainous north. Much of it is fertile farmland. The Snake River and its tributaries provide hydroelectric power for many small towns that dot the landscape. Water from the river also irrigates farm fields. Most people in Idaho live in the southern part of the state.

Idaho has more than 107,000 miles (172,200 km) of rivers, and more than 2,000 named lakes. Coeur d'Alene and Pend Oreille are large, beautiful lakes in the mountainous northern panhandle.

Coeur d'Alene Lake is a popular sports destination for residents and tourists. It is 25 miles (40 km) long and has more than 109 miles (175 km) of shoreline.

CLIMATE AND
WEATHER

Idaho is more than 300 miles (483 km) from the Pacific Ocean, but the state's climate is affected by ocean breezes. Warm, humid air drifts over Idaho, especially in winter. This helps make winter temperatures milder than in neighboring states such as Montana and Wyoming. Summers in Idaho are hotter and drier.

The hottest temperature ever recorded in Idaho was a blistering 118°F (48°C). It happened on July 28, 1934, in the central panhandle town of Orofino. Idaho's record cold temperature was a bone-chilling -60°F (-51°C) on January 18, 1943. It occurred at Island Park in east-central Idaho, near the border of Wyoming's Yellowstone National Park.

Because Idaho has so many mountains, the amount of rain and snow each region receives varies greatly. Some areas are drenched with 40 to 50 inches (102 to 127 cm) of precipitation each year. Other areas on the southern plateau receive less than 10 inches (25 cm). In the dry, summer months, wildfires are sometimes a danger in these desert-like regions. Statewide, the average amount of annual precipitation is 24 inches (61 cm).

Nampa, Idaho, residents stay cool in the summer at a downtown water fountain.

Snow blankets the University of Idaho in Moscow, Idaho.

CLIMATE AND WEATHER

PLANTS AND
ANIMALS

Trees seem to be everywhere in Idaho, especially in the rugged mountain areas. About 42 percent of this large state is forested. In northern Idaho, many of the mountains are covered in pine forests. The western white pine is the official state tree. Other common northern forest trees include towering white fir and Douglas fir. In southern forests, the most common trees include Douglas fir, lodgepole pine, and ponderosa pine. On the lower slopes of the mountains grow aspen, willow, mountain ash, maple, and birch trees.

**Evergreen Trees and
Mountain Syringa**

Long-Billed Curlew

A long-billed curlew stands in a field of wildflowers in Teton Valley, Idaho. Curlews use their long bills to poke into sand or mud for food such as crabs, grasshoppers, beetles, and other insects.

Wildflowers bloom in Idaho in the spring and summer. They include buttercups, lilies, and violets. The state flower is the syringa. It is also called the mock orange because of its sweet fragrance.

Idaho has several unique ecosystems. They range from mountains to lush valleys to arid sagebrush plains. The state includes millions of acres of unspoiled wilderness. People and roads are scarce. Most animals prefer to avoid humans, so naturally Idaho is filled with many kinds of mammals, birds, reptiles, and fish.

PLANTS AND ANIMALS

Grizzly Bear

Idaho is one of the few states where grizzly bears, mountain lions, and gray wolves still roam. Grizzly bears are an endangered species. They are found mainly in meadows and forests in northern Idaho and in the eastern part of the state bordering Wyoming's Yellowstone National Park.

Other common large mammals in Idaho's plains and mountains include elk, bighorn sheep, mountain goats, mule deer, and moose. On the plains of the Snake River roam deer, pronghorns, wolverines, and lynx.

There are many small mammals living throughout the state. They include skunks, squirrels, rabbits, raccoons, beavers, and otters.

Bald Eagle

Because of its many forests and wetlands, Idaho is often called a bird-watcher's paradise. Species seen flying through Idaho skies include whooping cranes, grouse, peregrine falcons, owls, ducks, swans, egrets, and bald eagles. American white pelicans can be found in the southeastern part of the state along the Snake River.

Idaho is famous for its fishing. The state's thousands of miles of cold streams and rivers are perfect breeding grounds for steelhead and cutthroat trout. Chinook and coho salmon spend most of their lives in the Pacific Ocean and then return to Idaho to spawn. Other fish found in the state's rivers and lakes include rainbow trout, brown trout, steelhead trout, black crappie, northern pike, white sturgeon, bluegill, catfish, smallmouth and largemouth bass, walleye, and perch.

HISTORY

Early Native Americans lived in present-day Idaho for at least 10,000 years. Archaeologists have found stone tools inside southern Idaho's Wilson Butte Cave. The tools are clues that humans used the cave as shelter after the last Ice Age.

During the 1700s, several Native American tribes lived in the Idaho area. In the north were the Nez Percé, the Salish, the Kootenai, and the Coeur d'Alene tribes. In the west-central region were the Northern Paiute. In the southern areas lived the Western Shoshone and the Northern Shoshone tribes. Some of these many tribes hunted game and traveled around the area by horseback. Others settled in one place, usually near major rivers. By 1800, approximately 8,000 Native Americans lived in Idaho.

A Nez Percé chief.

The Lewis and Clark Expedition first traveled through today's Idaho in 1805.

The first Americans of European descent to visit Idaho were probably members of the Lewis and Clark Expedition in 1805. Meriwether Lewis and William Clark were exploring the new territory of the Louisiana Purchase and lands beyond. On their way to the Pacific Ocean, the expedition traveled through Idaho. They met Shoshone, Salish, and Nez Percé Native Americans, and crossed the treacherous Bitterroot Mountains.

Soon after the Lewis and Clark Expedition passed through Idaho in 1805, trappers and hunters arrived. Idaho was rich with natural resources that attracted businesses. In 1809, the British (later Canadian) North West Company set up a trading post along the shores of Pend Oreille Lake, in northern Idaho. It was the earliest settlement of European Americans in Idaho. More trading posts were built along the Snake River in southern Idaho. Soon, trappers and missionaries moved into the region.

In the 1840s, settlers in wagon trains passed through Idaho on their way to California and Oregon. In 1860, gold was discovered on the Clearwater River in the northern panhandle. The precious metal was discovered in other places in the following years.

A prospector pans for gold in Idaho's Boise Basin in the 1800s.

A successful potato harvest on a ranch near Rupert, Idaho. The southern Idaho area became known as the Magic Valley. In the early 1900s, irrigation canals channeled water from the Snake River to "magically" create excellent farmland.

The population grew as prospectors and settlers poured in. Most did not strike it rich, but by 1863, almost 17,000 people had settled in Idaho. That same year, Idaho Territory was formed. Some farmers began planting potatoes, which thrived in the rich soil.

As more settlers arrived, the Native American tribes tried to stop the loss of their land. Many refused to move to reservations. They were also angry about broken treaties. They fought battles with the U.S. Army from the 1850s until the 1870s. By the late 1870s, the defeated Idaho tribes were forced to move to reservations, and white settlers claimed their lands.

In the late 1800s, Idaho continued growing. Railroad tracks were laid across the land, spurring the economy. The railroads made it easier for new settlers to arrive, and for goods to be sold and moved long distances. Lead and silver mines were dug out of the mountains, and sheep and cattle ranches appeared in the valleys and flatlands.

In 1909, workers rode the first train to go through the Bitterroot Mountains.

Many small farming towns sprang up, especially along the plains of the Snake River in southern Idaho. In 1889, the University of Idaho was founded in the city of Moscow, in the northwestern part of the state.

In 1890, Idaho became the 43rd state to join the United States. During the early 1900s, hydroelectric dams used river water to make electricity. Water was also diverted to irrigate farmland. Idaho became a leading agricultural state, helping feed troops during World War I (1914-1918). Logging also boomed in the state.

After suffering through hard times during the Great Depression of the 1930s, Idaho farmers once again helped feed the nation during and after World War II (1939-1945). Idaho factories made airplanes and other war supplies. Metals from Idaho's mines boosted the state and national economies.

In the last half of the 1900s and into the 2000s, Idaho's manufacturing industry expanded. Today, manufacturing, agriculture, and tourism are the biggest parts of Idaho's economy. The people of Idaho continue to find a balance between developing their precious land and preserving it for the future.

DID YOU KNOW?

- Craters of the Moon National Monument & Preserve is in southern Idaho. It contains three vast lava flows that occurred between 15,000 and 2,000 years ago. The volcanic eruptions cover more than 1,100 square miles (2,849 sq km) of land. It is a barren place filled with volcanic craters and weird lava flows frozen solid in time. Some of NASA's Apollo astronauts (Alan Shepard, Edgar Mitchell, Joe Engle, and Eugene Cernan) trained at Craters of the Moon in 1969. They learned about the area's volcanic geology to prepare for their Moon missions.

- Spectacular Shoshone Falls is part of the Snake River in southern Idaho, near the city of Twin Falls. It is 212 feet (65 m) high, which is 45 feet (14 m) taller than New York's Niagara Falls.

- Hells Canyon is one of the deepest river gorges in North America. It is located in the Seven Devils Mountain Range. At its deepest point, the canyon wall plummets 7,993 feet (2,436 m) to the Snake River far below, deeper than even Arizona's Grand Canyon.

Japanese immigrants imprisoned at Idaho's Minidoka Relocation Center in 1942.

- During World War II (1939-1945), fear gripped the nation. People panicked after the Japanese attack on Hawaii's Pearl Harbor naval base on December 7, 1941. Many believed that Japanese immigrants, even those who had become U.S. citizens, would help Japan and hurt America. More than 120,000 people of Japanese ancestry living on the West Coast were forced from their homes and jobs. About 13,000 of them were imprisoned at Minidoka Relocation Center in south-central Idaho.

  Surrounded by barbed-wire fences and armed guards, the Japanese lived in wooden barracks. Weather conditions were harsh, and supplies for everyday living were scarce. Despite their treatment, most Japanese remained loyal to the United States. More than 1,000 Minidoka detainees volunteered for military service. Seventy-three died for their country, and two won the Congressional Medal of Honor.

  After the war, Minidoka Relocation Center was closed in 1945. Today, the area has been preserved as a national historic site. In 1946, Minidoka combat veterans met with President Harry Truman. "You fought not only the enemy," the president said, "but you fought prejudice—and you have won."

PEOPLE

Gregory "Pappy" Boyington (1912-1988) was a United States Marine Corps fighter ace pilot during World War II (1939-1945). He was born in Coeur d'Alene, but spent much of his early childhood in St. Maries, Idaho. Boyington joined the Marine Corps in 1935 and soon began training to become a military aviator.

In 1941, Boyington joined the famed Flying Tigers, defending China from Japanese attack. In 1942, he was promoted to the rank of major. The following year, he organized Marine Fighter Squadron 214, better known as the Black Sheep Squadron. He shot down between 26 and 28 enemy planes before being shot down himself. He spent a year in a Japanese prisoner of war camp. After the war ended, Boyington was promoted to lieutenant colonel and awarded the Congressional Medal of Honor in 1945.

Harmon Killebrew (1936-2011) was a Major League Baseball player who spent most of his career with the Minnesota Twins. He was born and grew up in Payette, Idaho. Baseball scouts were impressed by Killebrew's raw strength, which helped him hit many home runs. He signed with the Washington Senators in 1954 at age 17. (The Senators later moved and became the Minnesota Twins.) During Killebrew's 22-year career, he became one of the best power hitters in baseball history. He was nicknamed "Killer" because of his powerful swing. At the time of his retirement in 1975, he had hit 573 home runs, more than any other right-handed batter in MLB history. Killebrew was inducted into the Baseball Hall of Fame in 1984.

Edgar Rice Burroughs (1875-1950) wrote some of the most beloved adventure and fantasy novels of the 20th century. He also wrote many Western and historical novels. He was born in Chicago, Illinois, but spent many of his early years in Idaho, including a job at a ranch. In 1912, he published *Tarzan of the Apes*, about a boy who was raised by apes in the jungles of Africa. The Tarzan character was so popular that Burroughs wrote 24 sequels. Many were made into comic books, films, and television shows. Another successful Burroughs creation was John Carter, the science fantasy hero who first appeared in 1912's *A Princess of Mars*. Other popular Burroughs novels include *The Land That Time Forgot* and *At the Earth's Core*.

Picabo Street (1971-) was one of the best downhill skiers in the world during the 1990s. She was born in the small Idaho town of Triumph. She was named after a nearby town (pronounced "peek-a-boo"). She was skiing by the age of six at Sun Valley, the popular Idaho ski area. She made the U.S. Ski Team at age 17. She won a silver medal at the 1994 Olympic Winter Games in Lillehammer, Norway. She won World Cup women's downhill titles in 1995 and 1996. A serious knee injury almost sidelined her career. But in 1998, Street won the gold medal in the super giant slalom at the Olympic Winter Games in Nagano, Japan. Street retired from competitive skiing after the 2002 Olympic Winter Games in Salt Lake City, Utah.

CITIES

Boise is the largest city in Idaho. It is also the state capital. Boise has a population of 216,282. Its neighboring towns and suburbs bring the population of the area to more than 660,000. It is in the southwestern part of the state. French trappers probably named the city in the 1820s when they spotted the tree-lined Boise River and exclaimed, "La rivière boisée" (the wooded river). Today, Boise is home to many high-tech manufacturers, as well as lumber, food processing, and service companies. Boise State University is located in the city. It is also home to Zoo Boise, which features more than 200 animals from around the world, and the Aquarium of Boise, with more than 250 species of animals and marine life.

Idaho Falls is the largest city in southeastern Idaho. Its population is 58,691. In 1865, businessman Matt Taylor built a bridge over the Snake River to help travelers, new settlers,

Taylor's Crossing

and U.S. Army troops. It became known as Taylor's Crossing. A town soon sprang up near the bridge. It was called Eagle Rock. In 1891, the name was changed to Idaho Falls, which referred to the rapids near the bridge. Today, Idaho Falls is a health care center for southeastern Idaho. It also hosts agricultural trade groups, high-tech industries, retail stores, and tourism-related businesses. The nearby Idaho National Laboratory nuclear power testing lab is a major employer.

Pocatello is in southeastern Idaho. It is named after Chief Pocatello of the Native American Shoshone tribe. The city began in the early 1800s as a trading post for pioneers traveling along the Oregon Trail. It became known as the "Gateway to the West." Settlers poured into the area after

the discovery of gold in 1860. Railroads came through in the 1870s, which made it easier to transport goods. Ranchers, farmers, and other settlers soon followed, and the town grew. Today, Pocatello's population is 54,292. Major employers include health care, high-tech manufacturing, food processing, insurance, and government. The city is also home to Idaho State University. Outdoor sports such as mountain biking, kayaking, and cross-country skiing are popular activities.

The marina and beach at Coeur d'Alene is a popular destination for residents and tourists.

Coeur d'Alene is in the mountainous panhandle region of northern Idaho. The city was founded in 1878 as a trading post. Pronounced "core-da-lane," it was named by French-speaking fur traders after the Native Americans who lived in the area. The city grew as more fur traders, miners, and loggers arrived. Railroads came to the area in 1886, increasing the population even more. Today, the city has 47,912 residents. Nicknamed "Lake City," it is on the northern shore of 25-mile (40-km) -long Coeur d'Alene Lake, one of the most scenic lakes in the country. The city is a center for health care, manufacturing, lumber, mining, and education. In recent years, tourism has become a major employer and a big reason for the city's rapid growth.

TRANSPORTATION

Idaho's vast rugged wilderness areas sometimes make it difficult to travel. There are no interstate highways linking the northern and southern parts of the state. Interstate 90 goes east and west across the northern panhandle. In the south, Interstates 86 and 84 go mainly east and west across the plains of the Snake River. Interstate 15 goes north and south for a short distance through southeastern Idaho, starting in Pocatello and crossing into neighboring Utah.

Idaho's rugged wilderness limits the number of roads through the state.

A seaplane waits at a dock at Coeur d'Alene Lake.

Because the northern and southern parts of the state are not connected by interstate highways, air transportation is very important. Six commercial airports are in Idaho. Boise Airport is the largest. Other airports include Pocatello Regional Airport, Lewiston-Nez Perce County Airport, Idaho Falls Regional Airport, Magic Valley Regional Airport in Twin Falls, and Friedman Memorial Airport in Hailey.

There are more than 280 airports, airstrips, seaplane bases, and heliports in Idaho. Some are used by the United States Forest Service for jobs such as controlling forest fires.

Port of Lewiston

The port in the city of Lewiston is on the far western border of the state's panhandle. It is the farthest inland seaport for ships that service the West Coast of the United States. Barges carrying bulky cargo like grain, lumber, or manufactured goods travel 465 miles (748 km) down the Snake and Columbia Rivers to the Pacific Ocean.

Three major cargo-hauling railroads service Idaho. They include Burlington Northern Santa Fe, Union Pacific, and Canadian Pacific Railway. Amtrak's *Empire Builder* passenger train travels across the northern panhandle.

NATURAL
RESOURCES

Gold was discovered in Idaho in the 1860s. Miners and other settlers rushed into the area. Today, gold is no longer important to the state's economy. Instead, silver, lead, and many other metals are dug out of Idaho mines. Idaho is a leader in mining and processing valuable gypsum, cement, and clay. Phosphate mining is also a big industry. It is used to make fertilizers and other chemicals.

Approximately 22 million acres (9 million ha) of Idaho is open range. Rangeland is land outside of cities where cattle and other animals are permitted to roam and graze. Much of it is in southern Idaho. It includes grasslands, woodlands, and mountain meadows. Beef cattle are one of Idaho's most valuable products.

A truck is loaded with phosphate ore at a mine near Soda Springs, Idaho.

A logging operation harvests trees outside of Coeur d'Alene, Idaho. The state has about 22 million acres (9 million ha) of forestland.

Forestland covers about 22 million acres (9 million ha) of Idaho's land. About 4 million acres (1.6 million ha) are set aside as wilderness. National forests occupy about 40 percent of Idaho, more than any other state. Trees logged in Idaho forests include fir, hemlock, lodgepole pine, ponderosa pine, and spruce.

Almost 12 million acres (4.9 million ha) of Idaho is farmland, supporting about 25,000 farms. Idaho is the nation's top potato supplier. About one-third of all United States potatoes are grown in Idaho. If Idahoans had to consume all the potatoes they grew, every person would have to eat 40 each day! Other leading Idaho agricultural products include milk, wheat, barley, Austrian winter peas, beans, and sugar beets.

NATURAL RESOURCES

INDUSTRY

Idaho's economy has changed and grown many times in its history. In the early 1800s, fur trapping by mountain men was the area's first big industry. In the 1860s, gold mining became important and brought many settlers to Idaho. As the plains of southern Idaho became irrigated with water from the Snake River, agriculture boomed. In the 1900s, timber harvesting helped the economy grow.

Today, agriculture, mining, logging, food processing, and manufacturing are all big Idaho industries. The state's most valuable farm products are beef cattle and milk. Food processing employs many people. Potatoes, sugar beets, wheat, beans, and meat are processed and packaged for sale all around the country as well as internationally.

Cattle graze on an Idaho ranch.

Idaho has diversified its economy. It no longer relies only on mining, logging, and agriculture. Many electronics and machinery companies have moved into the state, employing thousands of Idahoans and boosting the economy.

In recent years, tourism has boomed in Idaho as people have discovered the state's natural beauty and millions of square miles of unspoiled wilderness. Central Idaho's Sun Valley is world famous for skiing. Coeur d'Alene, in the northern panhandle, is a popular resort destination.

SPORTS

There are no major league sports teams in Idaho. However, there are several minor league teams where young players get valuable experience before hopefully moving up to the majors. The Boise Hawks and Idaho Falls Chukars are minor league baseball teams. The Idaho Stampede is a basketball team that plays home games in Boise. The Idaho Steelheads, also from Boise, play minor league hockey.

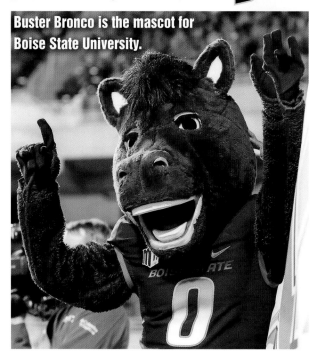

Buster Bronco is the mascot for Boise State University.

Idaho has several college teams that play in the National Collegiate Athletic Association (NCAA). The Boise State Broncos play for Boise State University. The Broncos football team is especially popular. The Idaho Vandals play for the University of Idaho in Moscow. The Idaho State Bengals represent Idaho State University in Pocatello.

An angler displays her catch from the Kootenai River near Leonia, Idaho.

With millions of acres of unspoiled wilderness available, it is no surprise that outdoor sports are huge in Idaho. People come from all over the nation to hunt and fish in the state's backcountry. Moose, pronghorn, mountain goats, elk, bighorn sheep, black bears, and mountain lions are big-game trophy species. Chinook and coho salmon, steelhead trout, and sturgeon are prized fish taken from Idaho's many rivers and lakes.

Idaho has several national parks, forests, trails, and monuments, plus dozens of state parks. A small portion of Yellowstone National Park is in eastern Idaho. Craters of the Moon National Monument & Preserve has ancient volcanic lava flows to explore. All over Idaho, people enjoy camping, skiing, hiking, and nature watching.

ENTERTAINMENT

The Idaho State Historical Museum is in Boise. It was founded in 1907 as a "cabinet of curiosities." Today, it includes a collection of more than 250,000 objects that explore the state's colorful history, from the time of the Old West to present-day Idaho.

The Old Idaho Penitentiary in Boise was a prison from 1872 to 1973. Today, visitors can tour the cell blocks, gallows, and one of the country's largest collections of historical weapons.

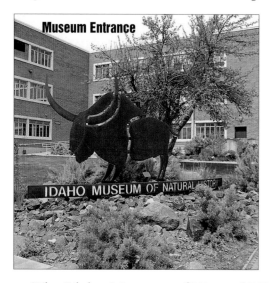

Museum Entrance

IDAHO MUSEUM OF NATURAL HISTORY

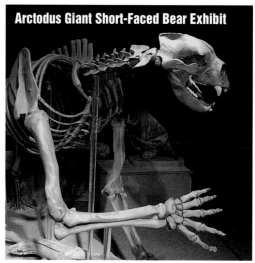

Arctodus Giant Short-Faced Bear Exhibit

The Idaho Museum of Natural History is in Pocatello. It features exhibits about Idaho geology, early people living on the Snake River Plain, and the plants and animals of southern Idaho.

Many of Idaho's larger cities and universities have orchestras, choirs, and theaters. Boise's Idaho Shakespeare Festival performs plays by William Shakespeare and others at an outdoor amphitheater along the shores of the Boise River during the summer months.

The McCall Winter Carnival is a week-long celebration, featuring music, parades, and snow sculptures such as this King Kong creation.

The North Idaho Fair & Rodeo is held each summer in Coeur d'Alene. It features thrill rides, musical acts, dancing, and the Pro-West Rodeo Finals. The McCall Winter Carnival is a week-long celebration with snow and ice sculptures, a torchlight parade, and live music.

The Bannock County Bluegrass Festival is held each year in Pocatello. Since 1967, the Lionel Hampton International Jazz Festival has been holding annual workshops and concerts at the University of Idaho in Moscow.

ENTERTAINMENT

TIMELINE

1700s—Several Native American tribes call this region home. These tribes include the Nez Percé, Kootenai, Salish, Coeur d'Alene, Northern Paiutes, and Shoshone.

1805—Meriwether Lewis and William Clark, with their expedition, explore the area.

1809—A trading post is set up on Pend Oreille Lake.

1840s—Wagon trains travel through Idaho on their way to California and Oregon.

1860—Gold is discovered on the Clearwater River.

1863—Idaho Territory is formed.

1874—The first railroad is built at Franklin, Idaho.

1890—Idaho becomes the 43rd state in the Union.

Early 1900s—Hydroelectric power plants are developed.

1906—The country's largest sawmill opens in Potlatch, Idaho.

1936—The Sun Valley resort opens. It features the country's first ski lift.

1939-1945—World War II helps Idaho economically.

1984—Idaho native Harmon Killebrew is elected to the Baseball Hall of Fame.

2009—The 2009 Special Olympics World Winter Games are held in Idaho.

GLOSSARY

Apollo Space Program

An American space exploration program that ran from 1963 to 1972. Run by the National Aeronautics and Space Administration (NASA), the program's goal was to land astronauts on the Moon and return them safely to Earth. The first Moon landing was achieved by Apollo 11 on July 20, 1969.

Arid

A very dry climate.

Great Depression

A time in American history beginning in 1929 and lasting for several years when many businesses failed across the country and millions of people lost their jobs.

Hydroelectric

A way of generating electricity that uses running water rather than burning oil or coal.

Kootenai

A Native American tribe living in Idaho, Washington state, and British Columbia, Canada, before European Americans arrived.

Lewis and Clark Expedition

An expedition led by Meriwether Lewis and William Clark, who explored the north and west parts of the United States from 1804 to 1806.

Louisiana Purchase

A purchase by the United States from France in 1803 of a huge section of land west of the Mississippi River. The United States nearly doubled in size after the purchase. The young country paid about $15 million for more than 828,000 square miles (2.1 million sq km) of land.

National Aeronautics and Space Administration (NASA)

A United States government agency started in 1958. NASA's goals include space exploration, as well as increasing people's understanding of Earth, our solar system, and the universe.

Nez Percé

A Native American tribe living in Idaho before the arrival of Europeans.

Panhandle

The narrow strip of land that is the northern section of Idaho.

Shoshone

A Native American tribe living in Idaho before the arrival of Europeans.

Wilderness

An area that has retained its natural beauty, untouched by human hands.

World War I

A war that was fought in Europe from 1914 to 1918, involving countries around the world. The United States entered the war in April 1917.

World War II

A conflict that was fought from 1939 to 1945, involving countries around the world. The United States entered the war after Japan bombed the American naval base at Pearl Harbor, in Oahu, Hawaii, on December 7, 1941.

INDEX